CATERPILLARS

CATERPILLARS

MARILYN SINGER

EarlyLight Books

WAYNESVILLE, NORTH CAROLINA, U.S.A.

Cataloging Information

Singer, Marilyn.

   Caterpillars/Marilyn Singer

        40 p. : col. ill. ; 25 cm.

   Includes index (p.).

   Summary: Explores the morphology and behavior of butterfly and moth caterpillars from around the world in verse and narrative. Includes a range of butterfly and moth species. Includes quiz, glossary, matching game, bibliographical references, and index.

   LC: QL 544

   Dewey: 595.78

   ISBN-13: 978-0-9797455-7-7 (alk. paper)

   ISBN-10: 0-9797455-7-8 (alk. paper)

JNF 595.78 caterpillars—juvenile literature

Cover & Interior Design: Cindy LaBreacht
Technical Reviewer: Dr. Louis Sorkin, American Museum of Natural History
Copy Editor: Susan Brill
Photo Research: Dawn Cusick

10 9 8 7 6 5 4 3 2 1; First edition

Published by EarlyLight Books, Inc.
1436 Dellwood Road, Waynesville, NC 28786, U.S.A.

ISBN 13: 978-0-9797455-7-7
ISBN 10: 0-9797455-7-8

TO LOU SORKIN, ENTOMOLOGIST EXTRAORDINAIRE

CATERPILLARS

Caterpillars smooth,
   Caterpillars hairy.
Munching in a giant bunch,
   Lunching solitary.

Caterpillars still,
   Caterpillars crawling.
Weaving through the twigs and leaves,
   Hanging without falling

Caterpillars plain,
   Caterpillars glowing.
Casting off their last tight skin.
   Every day they're growing.

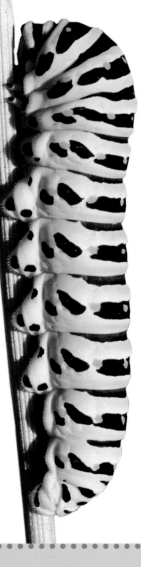

Caterpillars brave,
    Caterpillars rearing.
Hiding on a tree outside,
    Sometimes disappearing.

Caterpillars waiting
    Inside a new disguise.
Strangely changing, rearranging
    Right before our eyes,

Soon on wings they'll rise,
    Straight into the skies,
To spend their hours finding flowers—
    New moths and butterflies!

In your garden, in a rainforest, in a sack of flour, or on someone's wool sweater, a moth or a butterfly has laid her eggs. There are more than 100,000 kinds of moths and butterflies throughout the world. Some lay eggs one at a time. Others lay them in clusters. All of these eggs will hatch into *larvae*—babies that look totally different from their parents.

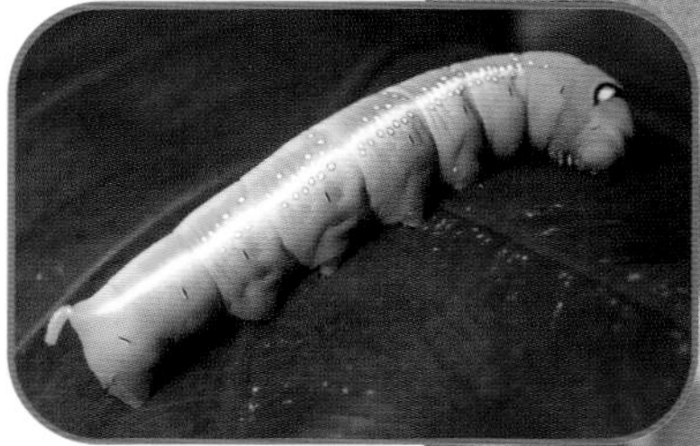

↑
A CATERPILLAR
IN THE SPHINX
MOTH FAMILY

CATERPILLARS SMOOTH...

TIGER MOTH WITH EGGS ↑

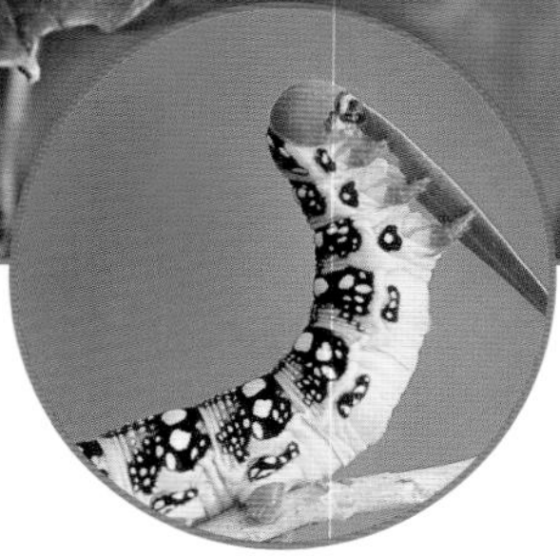

← SPURGE
HAWK MOTH

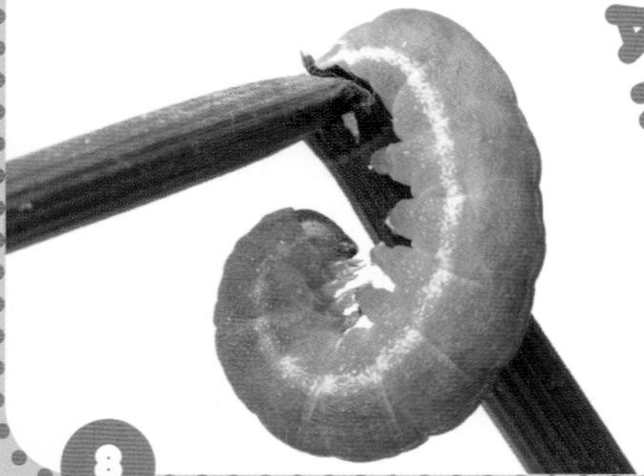

TUSSOCK MOTH →

← SPINY OAK SLUG CATERPILLAR

TIGER MOTH ↑

These babies will also look different from how they themselves will appear in a few weeks or months. Some will grow big and long; others will remain tiny. Some will have soft smooth skin. Others will be covered with fuzzy, silky, or bristly hairs, or with spikes to scare away birds and other hunters. A few will make you itch or burn your skin if you pick them up. Most will just tickle. None will have wings. All of them will be caterpillars.

CATERPILLARS HAIRY...

A caterpillar is born hungry. To hatch, it bites through its eggshell and then sometimes eats it. Its mother was careful to lay her eggs right on the larvae's favorite food so they can begin feeding right away.

Most adult moths and butter-flies drink *nectar*—flower or fruit juice. When they are caterpillars, they have a different diet. Caterpillars find their food by sight and smell. The majority eat leaves and other parts of plants, but some feed on more unusual things. **Waxworms**, the larvae of wax moths, are caterpillars that are born in bee hives. They eat honey and wax. **Clothes moth** caterpillars eat wool and other natural fabrics. They chew holes in our sweaters and carpets.

← MONARCH CATERPILLARS HATCHING FROM EGGS

A GROUP OF CATERPILLARS THAT LIVE SOCIALLY ↑

← CLOTHES MOTH

MUNCHING IN A GIANT BUNCH,

Some caterpillars live together, while others live alone. **Tent** caterpillars take shelter as a big group inside web nests that they spin from silk. They leave the nests as a group, too, when it's time to eat. **Gypsy moth** caterpillars also dine together. They are pests that can strip the leaves from whole forests. Other *species*—types— of caterpillars also destroy crops and trees. But birds and other *predators*—hunters— such as frogs, lizards, snakes, and mice eat these pests and help protect the plants.

MONARCH ↑

↑ LACKEY MOTH

For some caterpillars, such as the **monarch**, living alone makes it easier to hide from enemies. For other caterpillars, living together means that a number of caterpillars are bound to survive—no predator could devour such a big group.

In cool or mild places, most garden caterpillars don't travel very far. They move slowly over plants, eating the leaves. They don't waste any energy— they put it all into growing. When they're not eating, they rest under the leaves or beneath the plant. A lot of them will become adults before summer's end. But others will remain larvae for many months.

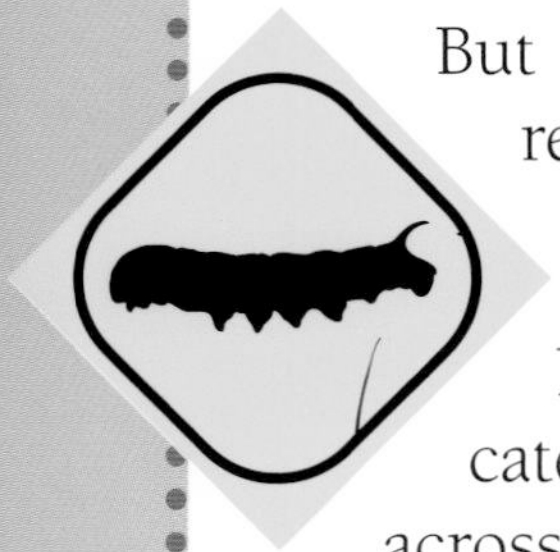

In autumn, some caterpillars crawl across roads and sidewalks to find a place to spend the winter.

A CATERPILLAR IN THE ↑
OWLET MOTH FAMILY

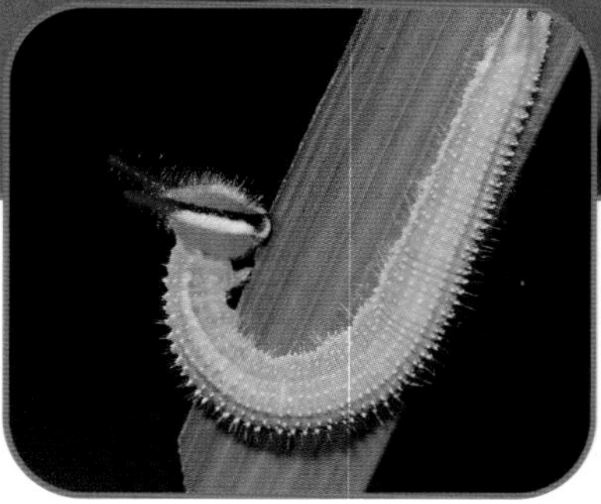

← A SPECIES OF
SATYRINE
BUTTERFLY

CATERPILLARS STILL,

↓ YELLOW WOOLY BEAR

↑ WOOLY BEAR

TIGER MOTH →

The **woolly bear** searches for a rock or a log to hide beneath, safe from the cold and from enemies. It can crawl four feet per minute. For a caterpillar, that's speedy!

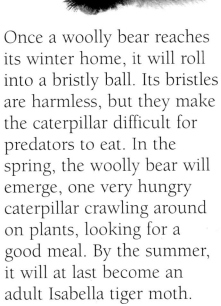

Once a woolly bear reaches its winter home, it will roll into a bristly ball. Its bristles are harmless, but they make the caterpillar difficult for predators to eat. In the spring, the woolly bear will emerge, one very hungry caterpillar crawling around on plants, looking for a good meal. By the summer, it will at last become an adult Isabella tiger moth.

CATERPILLARS CRAWLING...

A caterpillar can not only crawl. It can hang upside down or right-side up with ease. Like all insects, a caterpillar has six true legs in the thorax—the front part of its body. These will be its only legs when the caterpillar changes into a moth or butterfly. Most caterpillars also have ten stubby rear legs with hooks on the bottom. These are called *prolegs*. They help the caterpillar crawl and also cling to a branch or a leaf.

BLACK SWALLOWTAIL ↑

COXCOMB PROMINENT ↑

↑
ANOTHER SPECIES OF PROMINENT MOTH

WEAVING THROUGH THE TWIGS AND LEAVES,

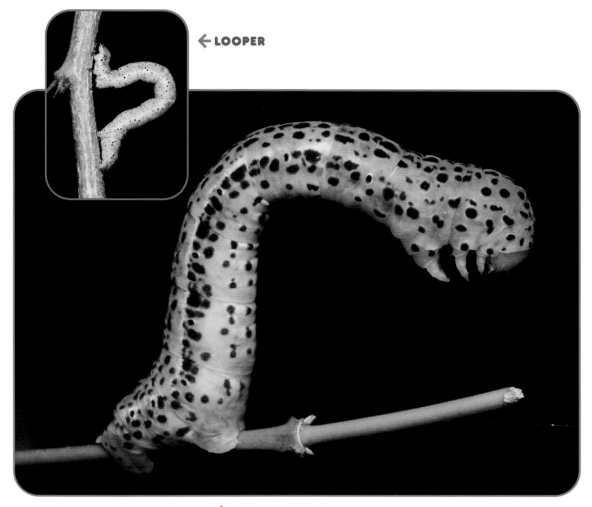

← LOOPER

DYSPHANIA MILITARIS ↑
INCHWORM

Loopers are missing two or three pairs of legs in the middle of their bodies. To move, they hump up and creep along inch by inch. That's why we call them **inchworms**, even though they're really caterpillars and not worms at all.

↑ LOOPER

HANGING WITHOUT FALLING.

Butterflies and moths come in amazing colors. So do caterpillars. Ones such as the **codling moth** caterpillar and the **Mexican jumping bean** caterpillar that live in and feed on seeds, fruit, or vegetables are mostly pale and colorless. But the **pandorus sphinx**, the **great peacock moth** caterpillar, and

↑ GIANT PEACOCK MOTH

many other caterpillars that live on plants, are often striped, spotted, marked, or banded. These patterns are sometimes so bright and strange that they look painted on their bodies.

Some caterpillars, including the **monarch**, the **gulf fritillary**, and the **queen**, use their bright colors to warn hunters that they taste bad. Others have *eyespots* — markings that look like eyes — bristles, or horns that startle enemies.

↑ PANDORUS SPHINX

CODLING MOTH →

CATERPILLARS PLAIN,

← TIGER SWALLOWTAIL

↑
← HICKORY
  HORNED
  DEVILS

← SPICEBUSH SWALLOWTAIL

The **tomato hornworm** has a single curved horn on its rear. It looks like a stinger, but it's harmless. The **hickory horned devil** appears even more frightening. It has spiky horns all over its body. But they are not dangerous either. It's safe to hold both of these species in your hands.

The **spicebush swallowtail** caterpillar's eyespots make it look like a small and scary snake. This caterpillar makes a shelter of leaves and spends the day there with just its head sticking out. Birds often mistake it for a reptile and leave the spicebush swallowtail alone.

CATERPILLARS GLOWING...

TOMATO HORNWORM →

As a caterpillar eats and grows, its skin or *exoskeleton* becomes too tight. It stops eating and *molts*—sheds this outer covering. Then it feeds again until its new skin is too tight and it must molt again. Each time a caterpillar sheds its skin, it begins a new stage called an *instar*.

Most types of caterpillars will generally pass through five or six instars.

MONARCHS MOLTING ↑

↑ CATALPA SPHINX MOLTING

CASTING OFF THEIR LAST TIGHT SKIN,

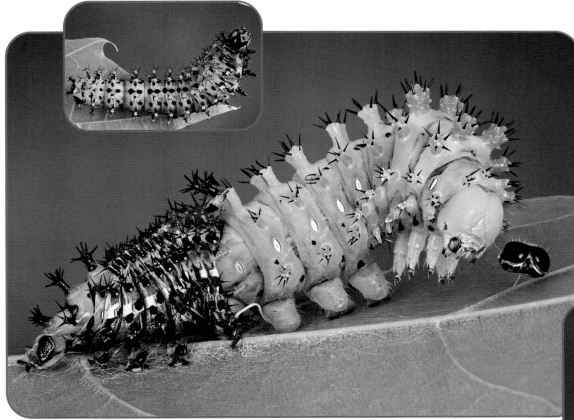

The first instar is when it hatches out of its egg as a tiny larva, and the last is before it is ready to change into a moth or butterfly. With each molt, a caterpillar's colors get brighter and its patterns become easier to see.

CECROPIA INSTARS BRIGHTENING AS THEY GROW

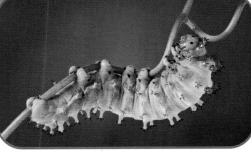

EVERY DAY THEY'RE GROWING.

Caterpillars' bright warning colors or patterns are not their only protection. The **oak leaf roller** will dangle out of danger from a silk thread and climb back up when the coast is clear. **Swallowtail** caterpillars, including the **Tiger**, **black**, and **spicebush**, raise a Y-shaped, reddish-orange scent gland called an *osmeterium* behind their heads. This gland gives off a nasty smell that repels predators, including parasitic wasps and flies—insects whose larvae feed on living caterpillars and eventually kill them.

Many **sphinx moth** caterpillars thrash around and throw up a sticky green fluid. Others, such as the **azalea** and **lobster** caterpillars, rear their heads and rear ends to look threatening. The **European puss moth** caterpillar not only raises its head, but it swings its rear end back and forth. If its bright red mask doesn't scare off the hunter, the caterpillar will spray burning acid in its enemy's face. For a bird, a puss moth is not a tasty treat.

← BLACK SWALLOWTAIL WITH ITS ORANGE OSMETERIUM

EUROPEAN PUSS MOTH ↑
EUROPEAN OAK LEAF ROLLER →

CATERPILLARS BRAVE,

← SADDLEBACK

↑ GRAY HAIRSTREAK
← IO

A large group of caterpillars, including **blues**, **harvesters**, **hairstreaks**, and **copper** butterflies, rely on ants to guard them from predators. The ants protect the caterpillars by spraying acid and biting enemies. In return for this protection, the caterpillars produce a sweet liquid for the ants to eat.

All caterpillars have *setae*—hairs—that allow them to sense touch. Some are covered all over with downy hairs. Still others have striking—but harmless—spines. A few, such as the **io** and the **saddleback** caterpillars, have spines that sting. The North American **puss moth** has long, soft hairs that make it look like a tiny, fluffy cat. But these hairs hide spines that inject *venom*—poison that can cause rashes, headaches, stomach problems, and fever. So beware of ever petting it!

↑ NORTH AMERICAN PUSS MOTH

CATERPILLARS REARING...

Caterpillars that taste bad don't mind being seen. Caterpillars that taste good do. So some caterpillars are good at *camouflage*—blending in with whatever they're sitting on.

JUNIPER HAIRSTREAK

A camouflaged caterpillar is hard to see. A **cabbageworm** is the same color as the food it eats. The **large maple spanworm** stretches out and lies still like a twig. Some kinds of **prominent moth** caterpillars appear to be dead leaves. They may even wave back and forth as if they were blowing in the wind.

MAPLE SPANWORM →

PROMINENT → MOTH

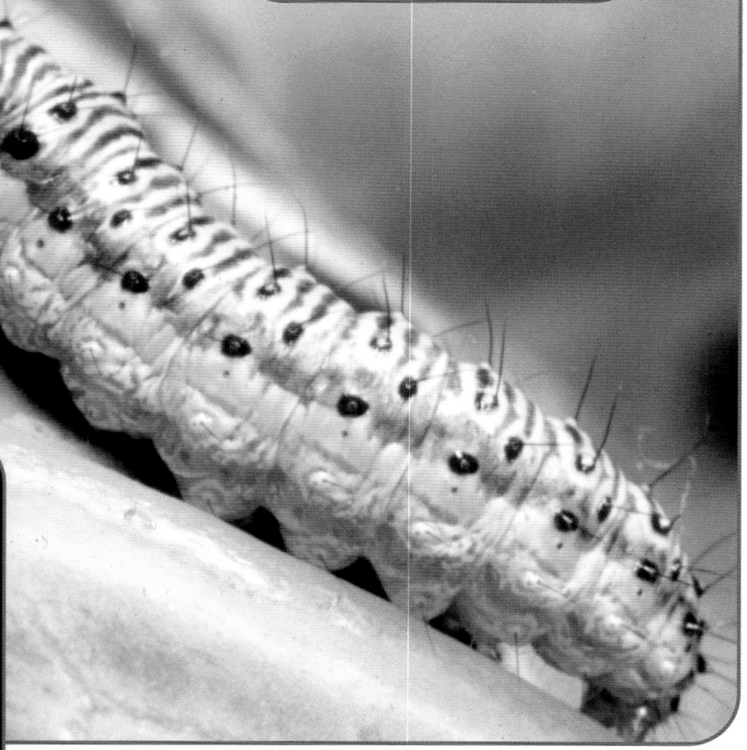

↑ CROSS-STRIPED CABBAGEWORM

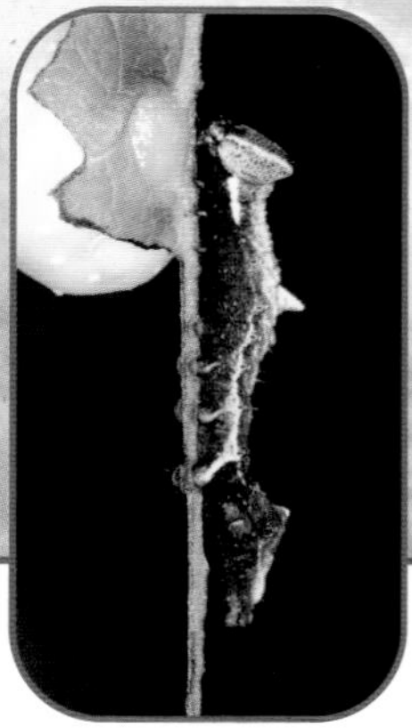

HIDING ON A TREE OUTSIDE,

WHITE ADMIRAL →

SPICEBUSH SWALLOWTAIL ↓

← VICEROY

↑
BAGWORM

Viceroy and **white admiral** caterpillars look like bird droppings. So do young **spicebush swallowtails**. But, by the fourth instar, these caterpillars resemble snakes instead.

Other caterpillars disappear by hiding in silk sacks they have made. Most **bagworms** camouflage these sacks with leaves and twigs. Inside these cases, the caterpillars will make their final and most dramatic change.

SOMETIMES DISAPPEARING.

If a caterpillar grows and molts and survives enemies and disease, it becomes a *pupa*—the stage between being a larva and an adult butterfly or moth. When it is about to *pupate*—become a pupa—the caterpillar finds a good place to rest. It might attach itself to a plant with hooks or a silk belt that it spins or it may bury itself among fallen leaves or underground. Its skin will shrink and split. It will become hard and still. It will never look like a caterpillar again.

↑
BORDERED PATCH CHRYSALIS

PAPER KITE CHRYSALIS →

MONARCH CHRYSALIS ↑
HUNGARIAN GLIDER CHRYSALIS → 

CATERPILLARS WAITING

A butterfly pupa is called a *chrysalis*, which comes from the Greek word for "gold" because quite a few chrysalises have golden spots. Butterfly caterpillars do not make *cocoons*. Many moth caterpillars do. Their silk is produced from glands near their mouthparts, which they spin around themselves. Sometimes the silk is mixed with hair or leaves. Some cocoons are considered valuable. People collect silkworm cocoons and spin them into silk thread used to make fine cloth.

FOREST TENT → CATERPILLAR PUPA IN LEAF

↑ FOREST TENT CATERPILLAR IN COCOON

INSIDE A NEW DISGUISE...

A pupa does not move. But inside its protective covering, it is going through amazing changes that we cannot see. Every bit of it is remade. It grows wings, lengthy antennae, and a tongue to drink nectar or water. Its six true legs become long and thin. This process is called *metamorphosis*. The changes may happen in just a few weeks or over many months until, at last, the moth or butterfly is ready to emerge.

CABBAGE LOOPER ↑

CLOUDLESS SULFUR ↑

BAGWORM→

STRANGELY CHANGING, REARRANGING

Butterflies wiggle around to split open the hard outer skin of the chrysalis. Some moth caterpillars chew a circle in the cocoon. When they are ready to emerge, they push it open.

Other types of moths cut their way out with a saw-like spine on their wings. Still others, such as the puss moth, use acid to dissolve the cocoon. Then they emerge to greet the world.

MONARCH → CHRYSALIS

↑ MONARCH BUTTERFLIES EMERGING

RIGHT BEFORE OUR EYES...

A brand-new moth or butterfly is wet and crumpled. It flaps its wings slowly to pump blood into them until they reach their full size. It keeps flapping until the wings are stiff and dry. In less than a few hours, it is ready to fly.

LUNA MOTH ↑

↑ YELLOW MIGRANT

SOON ON WINGS THEY'LL RISE

Away it will go to find a meal and a mate, to make more caterpillars that will fill us with wonder and delight.

↑ A SPECIES OF DANAID BUTTERFLY

↑ MONARCH

STRAIGHT INTO THE SKIES

TO SPEND THEIR HOURS FINDING FLOWERS...

↑ TIGER SWALLOWTAIL

NEW MOTHS AND BUTTERFLIES!

↑ SILVER-WASHED FRITILLARIES

31

POP QUIZ!

1. Most caterpillars eat:

   A. Bones
   B. Soap
   C. Leaves
   D. Candy
   E. Hotdogs with relish and mustard

2. How many true legs do caterpillars have— the only legs they'll have when they change into a moth or butterfly?

   A. 6
   B. 8
   C. 14
   D. 24
   E. 999

3. What is the advantage of living alone for a caterpillar? What is the advantage of living in a group?

4. Which is a caterpillar?

   A. Woolly bear
   B. Lobster caterpillar
   C. Inchworm
   D. Puss moth
   E. None of the above
   F. All of the above

5. What are eye spots and why do caterpillars have them?

6. **TRUE OR FALSE:** Some caterpillars, such as the monarch, have bright colors to warn enemies that they taste bad.

7. Which of these is not a type of self-defense that caterpillars use?

   A. Using stinging spines
   B. Biting with sharp teeth
   C. Giving off a bad smell
   D. Spraying acid in an enemy's face
   E. All of the above
   F. None of the above

8. Caterpillars shed their skins several times as they grow. This is called:

A. Bolting
B. Molting
C. Revolting
D. Vaulting
E. Waltzing

9. Caterpillars also use camouflage in self-defense. Which is NOT an example of caterpillar camouflage?

A. Looking like a twig
B. Looking like bird droppings (poop)
C. Looking like a leaf
D. Looking like the food it eats
E. Looking like a basketball

10. A pupa is:

A. A type of dangerous caterpillar
B. The stage between being an egg and being a caterpillar
C. The stage between being a caterpillar and being a moth or butterfly
D. A student in elementary school
E. All of the above

11. TRUE OR FALSE:
Butterflies make cocoons.

12. When caterpillars metamorphose— change into moths or butterflies— they develop:

A. Wings
B. Antennae
C. Tongues
D. All of the above
E. None of the above

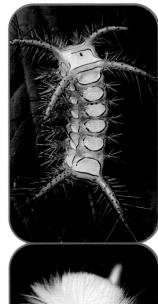

MATCH THE CATERPILLAR

1 CINNABAR

2 CROWNED SLUG

3 PUSS

4 LEOPARD

5 TOMATO HORNWOOM

6 TUSSOCK

7 LUNA

8 PEACOCK

9 ZEBRA LONGWING

TO THE MOTH OR BUTTERFLY

ANATOMY OF A CATERPILLAR

Like all insects, caterpillars have an *exoskeleton* and three body sections—the head, the *thorax* (middle), and the *abdomen* (the rear)—and three sets of jointed legs, found on the thorax. These are their true legs, and they will become long and thin when the caterpillars *metamorphose*—change into butterflies or moths. The remaining stubby prolegs on the abdomen will disappear.

Caterpillars have a heart, but no lungs. They breathe through small pores called *spiracles*. These may be seen as spots along the sides of a caterpillar's body. As larvae, they can detect changes in light through six pairs of simple eyes called *ocelli*. As adults, they have *compound eyes*—many eyes in one—to detect color and movement, and they can see objects in all directions at the same time. To sense smells, caterpillars have tiny *antennae*—feelers—near their mouths. These will develop into lengthy antennae which will not only allow them to taste and smell, but to help them balance as they fly. To sense touch, caterpillars have *setae* on their bodies. Adults have these hairs on their bodies, too, including their wings.

Since a caterpillar's job is to eat a lot and grow, it has strong *mandibles*—jaws—to chew plant material. A few species are carnivorous—they eat soft-bodied insects and spiders. A butterfly or moth does not have jaws. It has a coiled feeding tube called a *proboscis* used like a straw for sipping nectar from flowers. Some moths have proboscises with barbs so that they can hook them in place to drink tears from sleeping birds. A few, nicknamed "vampire moths," can even pierce human skin with their proboscises to drink blood. They sound scary, but fortunately, they aren't especially harmful to us or other animals.

GLOSSARY

camouflage: the use of colors, patterns, and shape to blend into the surroundings and hide from enemies.

chrysalis: a butterfly pupa, particularly the hard case enclosing it.

cocoon: the case made of silk and sometimes other material that encloses a moth pupa.

exoskeleton: the outer covering of an insect. In caterpillars, before metamorphosis, it is soft and skin-like.

instar: a stage of a larva's life; each time it molts, it begins a new instar. A larva will generally pass through five instars.

larva: the young, wingless form of an insect. The plural is **larvae**.

metamorphosis: the great change from a larva to an adult animal. A caterpillar **metamorphoses** into a moth or butterfly. Fish, amphibians, and other animals also metamorphose.

molt: to shed the outer skin or other coverings, such as hair or feathers, and replace these with new growth. Most larvae molt four times.

nectar: juice produced by a plant's flower or fruit.

osmeterium: the Y-shaped defense organ that some caterpillars have on their heads. It releases a bad smell to chase off predators.

predator: a hunter. The animal that it captures and eats is its prey.

prolegs: a larva's additional stubby legs that aid in climbing and clinging; they are not true legs because they aren't jointed. A moth or butterfly will not have prolegs.

pupa: an insect's stage between larva and adult during which it undergoes metamorphosis in a protective covering. The plural is pupas or pupae. When a caterpillar turns into a pupa, it **pupates**.

setae: hairs used to sense touch, and, in some cases, to inject venom.

venom: poison that is injected, generally by means of spines, fangs, or stingers.

FOR MORE INFORMATION

BOOKS

Allen, Thomas J, James P. Brock, and Jeffrey
   Glassberg, *Field Guide to Caterpillars*,
   New York: Oxford University Press, USA, 2005.

Carter, David, *Field Guide to the Caterpillars
   of Britain and Europe,* London: Collins, 2001.

Facklam, Margery, *Creepy, Crawly, Caterpillars,*
   Boston: Little, Brown, 1999.

Gibbons, Gail, *Monarch Butterfly*, New York:
   Holiday House, 1989.

Heligman, Deborah, *From Caterpillar to Butterfly*,
   New York: HarperCollins, 1996.

Latimer, Jonathan P. and Karen Stray Nolting,
   Young Naturalist Guide to Caterpillars, Boston:
   Houghton Mifflin Harcourt, 2000.

Murawski, Darlyne, *Face to Face with Caterpillars*,
   Washington D.C.: National Geographic, 2007.

Pringle, Laurence, An Extraordinary Life:
   The Story of the Monarch Butterfly, New York:
   Orchard Books, 1997.

Ryder, Joanne, *Where Butterflies Grow*, New York:
   Dutton, 1989.

Wagner, David L., *Caterpillars of Eastern North
   America*, Princeton, New Jersey: Princeton
   University Press, 2005.

Wright, Amy Bartlett, *Peterson First Guide
   to Caterpillars of North America*, Boston,
   Houghton Mifflin Harcourt, 1998.

WEB RESOURCES

On moths and butterflies:

http://butterflywebsite.com/index.htm
http://www.centralamerica.com/cr/butterfly/

On caterpillars:

http://extension.missouri.edu/publications/DisplayPub.aspx?P=IPM1019#life
http://www.enchantedlearning.com/subjects/butterfly/anatomy/Caterpillar.shtml
http://animals.howstuffworks.com/insects/caterpillar.htm
http://www.butterfly-guide.co.uk/life/
http://lepidoptera.butterflyhouse.com.au/
http://www.learnaboutbutterflies.com/Caterpillar%20thumbs.htm
http://www.ca.uky.edu/entomology/entfacts/ef003.asp
http://www.ag.auburn.edu/enpl/bulletins/caterpillar/caterpillar.htm

On conserving insects and other invertebrates:

http://www.xerces.org/
http://extension.missouri.edu/publications/DisplayPub.aspx?P=IPM1019#life
http://www.enchantedlearning.com/subjects/butterfly/anatomy/Caterpillar.shtml
http://animals.howstuffworks.com/insects/caterpillar.htm

On stinging caterpillars:

http://www.ca.uky.edu/entomology/entfacts/ef003.asp
http://www.ag.auburn.edu/enpl/bulletins/caterpillar/caterpillar.htm

Conserving insects and other invertebrates:

http://www.xerces.org/

SCIENTIFIC/COMMON NAMES

There are more than one and a half million known species in the world. Scientists from many countries are able to communicate with each other by giving these different species scientific names in Latin. They use a structure with a set of categories to classify animals. This is called *taxonomy*. Taxonomy shows how groups of creatures are similar to each other. In animal taxonomy, the first and biggest category to include butterflies and moths, as well as other animals, is *domain*. The last three categories are *family, genus* and *species*. There are also sub-families and sub-species when animals live in the same general area, but have some differences in behavior or anatomy. Families have things in common with each other, but they also have a number of differences. Species have the most things in common with each other and they can mate and produce fertile offspring.

In the text of this book, we use mostly the common English names for the caterpillars (except in cases where they don't have common English names or we don't know the common names). Here are the scientific names for the butterflies and moths mentioned in this book.

BUTTERFLIES
Black swallowtail: *Papilio polyxenes*
Blues: Polyommatinae (subfamily)
Bordered patch: *Chlosyne lacinia*
Cloudless sulfur: *Phoebis senna*
Cross-striped cabbageworm:
    Evergestis rimosalis
Coppers: Lycaeninae (subfamily)
Gray hairstreak: *Strymon melinus*
Gulf fritillary: *Agraulis vanillae*
Hairstreaks: Theclinae (subfamily)
Harvesters: Miletinae (subfamily)
Hungarian glider: *Neptis rivularis*
Juniper hairstreak: *Callophrys gryneus*
Monarch: *Danaus plexippus*
Paper kite: *Idea leuconoe*
Queen: *Danaus gilippus*
Silver-washed fritillary: *Argynnis paphia*
Spicebush swallowtail: *Papilio troilus*
Tiger swallowtail: *Papilio glaucus*
Viceroy: *Limenitis archippus*
White admiral: *Limenitis arthemis*
Yellow migrant: *Catopsilia gorgophone*
Zebra longwing: *Heliconius charitonius*

MOTHS
Azalea: *Datana major*
bagworms: Psychidae (family)
Cabbage looper: *Trichoplusia ni*
Catalpa sphinx: *Ceratomia catalpae*
Cecropia: *Hyalophora cecropia*
Cinnabar: *Tyria jacobaeae*
Clothes moth: *Tineola bisselliella*
Cross-striped cabbageworm:
    Evergestis rimosalis
Crowned slug moth: *Isa textula*
Codling: *Cydia pomonella*
Coxcomb prominent:
    Ptilodon capucina
European oak leaf roller:
    Tortrix viridana
Forest tent caterpillar:
    Malacosoma disstria
Great peacock moth: *Saturnia pyri*
Gypsy: *Lymantria dispar*
Hickory horned devil (Royal walnut
    moth): *Citheronia regalis*
Io: *Automeris io*
Lackey: *Malacosoma neustria*

Large maple spanworm:
    Prochoerodes lineola
Leopard moth: *Hypercompe scribonia*
Lobster moth: *Stauropus fagi*
Loopers: Geometridae (family)
Luna: *Actias luna*
Mexican jumping bean moth:
    Laspeyresia saltitans
Owlet moths: Noctuiidae (family)
Pandorus sphinx: *Eumorpha pandorus*
Prominents: Notodontidae (family)
Puss moth (European): *Cerura vinula*
Puss moth (North American):
    Megalopyge opercularis
Saddleback: *Acharia stimulea*
Sphinx moths: Sphingidae (family)
Spiny oak slug moth: *Euclea delphinii*
Spurge hawk moth: *Hyles euphorbiae*
Tiger moths: Arctiidae (family)
Tomato hornworm (Five-spotted
    hawk moth): *Anduca quinquemaculata*
Tussock moths: Lymantriidae (family)
Waxworms: Pyralidae (family)
Woolly bear (Isabella moth):
    Pyrrharctia isabella

INDEX

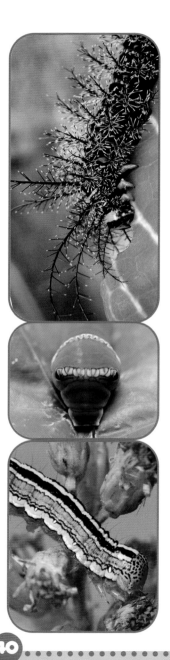

ACKNOWLEDGMENTS

The following individuals and organizations generously allowed their images to be reproduced: David Cappaert (page 23), Michigan State University, Bugwood.org; Clemson University - USDA Cooperative Extension Slide Series (page 32), Bugwood.org; Whitney Cranshaw (page 26), Colorado State University, Bugwood.org; Jerald E. Dewey (page 25), USDA Forest Service, Bugwood.org; Chris Evans (page 6), River to River CWMA, Bugwood.org; Howard Ensign Evans (page 35), Colorado State University, Bugwood.org; John H. Ghent (page 19), USDA Forest Service, Bugwood.org; Lacy L. Hyche (pages 26, 34, 35), Auburn University, Bugwood.org; Steven Katovich (pages 16 and 25), USDA Forest Service, Bugwood.org; Louis-Michel Nageleisen (page 20), Département de la Santé des Forêts, Bugwood.org; James Solomon (page 35), USDA Forest Service, United States, Bugwood.org; USDA Forest Service—Northeastern Area Archive (page 23), USDA Forest Service, Bugwood.org; Ronald Ham (page 40).

Many thanks to Steve Aronson and Michele Coppola, to Dr. James Costa and Dr. David Wagner for species identification assistance, and to my wonderful editor, Dawn Cusick.